A ZOMBIE'S GUIDE TO BEING DEAD

A ZOMBIE'S GUIDE TO BEING DEAD

A guide to surviving *and* enjoying the afterlife!

Djinn Publishing

Printed in the United States of America

ISBN 978-0-9949398-1-4

Djinn Publishing
2956 16th ave E.
Vancouver BC
Canada
www.djinnpublishing.com

Ordering Information:
Quantity sales. Special discounts are available on quantity purchases by corporations, associations, and others. For details, contact the publisher at the address above. Orders by U.S. trade bookstores and wholesalers. Please place orders here;
https://www.createspace.com/pub/l/createspacedirect.do

Djinn Publishing

CONTENTS

FOREWARD

When I first received BRUUUGGGHHHHH's submission, my initial reaction was that it was a joke.

I'd never heard of a zombie writing a book. The thought was laughable. I had always thought that they were brainless killing machines as we are led to believe in the media.

Then there was the state of her manuscript. It was an utter mess.

I nearly threw the whole thing out but luckily, before I did that, I read her query letter.

BRUUUGGGHHHHH outlined the struggles that she had gone through in her afterlife and then briefly explained the changes that she had made. She said that she wanted to change the way people thought of zombies and she wanted more than anything, to make a difference.

It was such a heartfelt letter that I had to give her a chance.

The first few pages were extremely difficult to read through, but I stuck to it and eventually learned to get into the groove and see past all of the spelling and grammar issues.

That was when I realized, she was the real deal. She is a strong, passionate, driven undead person and I have to say that if we didn't publish her book, someone else would have.

Through the editing process, I saw firsthand how driven and hardworking BRUUUGGGHHHHH is. Her passion is contagious and I am so proud to have been a part of this book. I hope that whether you are living or undead, A Zombie's Guide to Being Dead opens your eyes to a very different world that many are living in today.

INTRODUCTION

I can only assume that most people who pick up this book are undead, just like me. Perhaps, until recently, you weren't any type of dead at all and you aren't dealing with this turn of events very well. *Or* perhaps you have been undead for quite some time already, and are finally looking for some way to prolong and enjoy your life.

No matter your reason, the time has come for change. Why else would you pick up a book and force rotting, dried eyes to read the small words on this page.

Well, let me just start by telling you; **you have made the right choice.**

My name is Cassidy Heart. Or it was once before. Now, if anyone asks, I mostly go by BRUUUGGGHHHHH.

Let me tell you a little bit about myself and *why* I decided to write this book.

In life, I made it to the ripe age of twenty-seven. I studied interior design at CSU, had a banging apartment and a group of models, makeup artists and designers as friends. I use the term "friends" lightly, because although they were my die hard group of girls for GNO or gossiping about the hot new so-and-so in the neighborhood, the moment that I passed away, everything changed between us.

The rigor mortis was a bit hard to grasp at the beginning and my hand just couldn't hit the elevator button no matter how many times I tried, so I actually stomped my way up twenty seven flights of stairs. It took me about two hours, but with perseverance, I got to the floor of my apartment.

I don't know what I was thinking; the door handle was impossible.

That was one of my first moments of understanding. Those of you out there who have also gone through the *transition* will know exactly what I mean.

I call it The Beacon Effect. It's like a bright light shines into your mind momentarily to show you how different you have become. TBE happened to me right then, standing at my apartment door and thinking; *hey, how were you planning to open the door anyway? You can barely move your arms, let alone your fingers.*

My only other option was Sally.

Sally lived down the hall and was one of my best friends. And she had just come from my funeral, so I guessed it would be a surprise to see me. A delightful surprise of course, like low calorie cheesecake. She would be delighted and pour me a large glass of wine and I could sink into her big white couch and forget about this ordeal for a while.

I dragged my feet to her door and swung my arms against it. I managed to make a dull thumping sound and waited, but no one seemed to hear.

Frustrated, I knocked my head against the door, banging it three times before stopping. I wondered if she would hear me. I heard talking inside, what sounded like Jess and Alana and Michelle and then *finally*, perky footsteps.

The door swung swiftly open.

I nearly fell inside.

Sally gasped and stepped back, her big eyes wide and staring at me. She was still in her black dress. Versace from *three* seasons ago.

That bitch.

"Cassidy?" she breathed.

"Hgggggguuuuuuuuuu," I replied.

Of course, I didn't mean to say that but my tongue was just so *heavy*. It slipped out of my mouth at the end and then just hung there in the air between us.

Sally's face contorted.

"Ew."

She slammed the door shut and that was it.

That was the end to my friendship. All of my friendships in fact, in one sweeping motion and the sound of a lock clicking into place.

Hah! Like I could have even opened that door.

I ended up spending a few days sitting in the stair well, contemplating my afterlife. Thoughts move slowly when your brain has been shut off and then turned half-back-on.

There I was, a young undead woman with no friends, unable to get into my apartment. Not to mention dealing with clients would be a nightmare, now that I couldn't talk.

Eventually, the hunger got to me and I was faced with two options. I could either embrace this second life that I was given, or I could allow myself to waste away, defeated.

Well let me tell you something; in life, Cassidy Heart was never defeated and in death, BRUUUGGGHHHHH wouldn't be either.

Now, it wasn't easy. I'm not saying that I skipped down those steps into the fresh LA air and became the number one zombie bitch on the block overnight. BUT through trial and error and a lot of hard work, I managed to find my stride in the afterlife, find a purpose and find happiness. And with these techniques that I will provide within this book, *you* can find all those things too.

Each chapter within this book, contains valuable information that I have compiled through my own observations of my body and my life, as well as the experiences of other zombies that I have spent time observing and getting to know.

Keep your eyes open for special tips, just like this one.

TIP

While reading, follow these steps;

1. **Blink! (It's easy to forget, but any rest for the eyes goes a long way.)**
2. **If your head starts to hurt, take a break! (This is supposed to be a positive experience, let's not ruin it by pushing our minds too far.)**
3. **If you start to get tired, take a break! (Don't use up all of your energy, it is precious.)**
4. **If your eyes hurt in *any* way, stop reading! (Reading can be too much of a strain on the eyes sometimes. It's not worth losing an eye or two. So if they feel sore, it's time to take a break and return to your spot another day.)**

CHAPTER ONE - Basic Mechanics

What you will learn in this chapter;
✓ What is a Zombie?
✓ How do we rise from the grave? (If we ever make it to one)
✓ How do we keep unliving? What is Regeneration?

What is a Zombie?

A zombie is a creature of the night, a creature of darkness, a threat to humanity, a bringer of doom.

Or so the living say.

In reality, zombies are people—after the "living" is over. No, we aren't supposed to be here anymore *technically*, but we are creatures of the earth, just like anyone else.

Zombie's once had a human life and they remember it. For whatever reason, the brain is the last thing to ever go for a zombie. Maybe you've seen the odd one walking into a wall or simply drooling and wasting away—those zombies are at the end of their unlives. Fresh, "healthy" zombies are more often chasing people, crawling to different locations or reliving the good old days by revisiting memorable places from their past lives.

For those living people reading this; we can *all* remember, we can *all* think. Unfortunately though, our motor skills aren't the best and yes, sometimes hunger blinds us.

How do zombies rise from the grave? (If we ever make it to one)

There are a few different methods, of course, as any movie buff will know.

The act of rising from the grave traditionally stemmed from what people consider black magic. **Voodoo curses** were used on specific individuals to reanimate and use primarily as slaves.

Despite the fact that Zombies raised by black magic tend to remain better preserved and more nimble, I'd take the loose skin and limp arms over being a slave any day, thank you very much.

More common now a days are cursed grounds. **Dark times**, demonic plagues and hell rising often leads to bouts of the dead rising all over the place.

> **TIP**
>
> **If you are a Dark Times zombie, pay extra attention to *Chapter Three – Walk Don't Run***

This method never seems to stick though. These particular zombies are much more fragile due to longer periods of time rotting in their graves. They don't often last very long, even with the natural regeneration that all zombies have.

If you are one such Zombie, you will require extra care in order to elongate your existence.

The most common type of zombies are those affected by a **Zombie Virus**, like what happened to me.

It often begins as a fever, develops into hallucinations and then swiftly kills you—only to wake you back up again, a moment later.

This virus is *highly contagious* so once turned, do your best to steer clear of loved ones.

I know it sounds extreme, but in my case, all it took was a little scratch to the arm. I barely even noticed that the woman I was standing next to at the Beverly Center looked an inch from death.

It was black Friday and I foolishly mistook the bloodlust in her eyes for discount-lust and went for the bag at the same time that she reached out and clawed me.

Sad, I know.

It would have been easy to spot if I was looking, but I'll stop there. This is not a book to teach how to avoid becoming a zombie. It is a book to teach how to embrace being one.

How Do We Keep Unliving? What is Regeneration?

The term regeneration is often thrown around quite casually but a lot of people don't really understand what it is.

Regeneration in zombies, is not in fact magic, as most might assume. It is the simple act of cells reproducing, much as they would in a living person's body.

Did you know? Brain cells don't divide. Could that be why we retain our human identities?

Cells divide and reproduce constantly while other cells die, maintaining the fragile balance of life.

But in the case of the zombie body, cells continue to die at the regular rate while those that regenerate do so at approximately half the rate.

This means a few *very interesting* things.

1. We are not immortal. We die too, BUT…
2. We can live up to two times longer than we would have if we remained "alive".
3. We are constantly in a state of dying.

I know. Technically everyone is *always* dying, but for us—coming back from *literally* being dead and then only reproducing some cells at half the rate—we are actually *decomposing*.

This little (big) issue, is what leads us into the importance of chapters two and three.

CHAPTER TWO - Brain on the Brain

What you will learn in this chapter;
✓ Why do you crave brain?
✓ How to overcome hunger and make valid choices
✓ Integrating into living society
✓ Alternative choices
✓ Dangers of the wilds

Why do we crave brain?

Since the **Dark Times** and **Virus** zombie's first appearances back in the nineteen-thirties, zombies have craved brain.

Over the years, many people have had theories; it regenerates our own brains, the brain is the tastiest part, zombies like to smash heads open, etc.

The first guess is incorrect, but close. The nutrients from human brains act as nourishment for our own brains, the way that fertilizer works in a garden. It offers us the chance to maintain our brain and feed it, in a way, so that for a short time after feeding, our heads clear a little, our motor skills sharpen—it's like having that morning coffee.

It's also fun to smash heads open and brain *is* delicious! But those are just the perks.

How to overcome hunger and make valid choices

This is the kicker. It is the most difficult hurdle to overcome and it is the most important…

STEP 1:

As a zombie, just like a person, you have to make choices. You have to look at yourself and decide exactly what type of afterlife you want to have.

There is nothing wrong with rampaging. If you would like to live a life in which you run like mad, chase down meals and cause havoc, I applaud you. It is who you are. In a way, it is who we all are. Have fun with it!

BUT be honest. Are you rampaging on auto pilot? Are you chasing people down because you're starving? Do you *want* to cut your afterlife short?

For me, the answer is no. It has always been no. I knew this immediately because, for one, I've never liked to break a sweat, even in life. No way am I running. I'm not ashamed to say that I like to look good and if I have to be undead, well then, I'm going to be the best maintained zombie in the city.

Looks aside, there is one other little thing to consider;

how comfortable do you want your life to be?

I don't want to be starving at any given time. Let's be honest, no one does. I also don't want the discomfort of a disability.

How many zombies are missing limbs? How much harder is their afterlife? It's hard to think that it could happen to you, but trust me, all of us undead are more prone to these types of things. Some may even say that it is inevitable. It very well may be, so why not maintain our bodies before it gets to that point.

Step one is to decide if you want to have a long afterlife.

If the answer is yes, you can follow step two.

STEP 2:

Don't chase anyone. EVER.

Easier said than done with *brain on the brain.*

The way people move when they're frightened, the flittering this way and that—almost like a butterfly—it compels us to chase them. In fact, it makes it nearly impossible not to. *Nearly.*

I'll share my story with you. It is pretty weird, a zombie that doesn't chase people down, but I have my reasons.

At about a month, maybe more, of being undead, I had already had my fair share of human brains and epic chases. On one such occasion, I barreled down an escalator at the mall and landed straight on top of my meal. The fall didn't hurt. It was actually fun and I got an easy lunch out of it.

I ate the brain and felt a thrill from the juices, the adrenaline and the excitement. TBE flushed me. At that moment, I truly enjoyed being a zombie.

Then, as the excitement faded, I noticed that some of the flesh before me was not ripe with blood. It was my own.

My arm had been skinned from the shoulder down to the elbow, bone and muscle were exposed.

It was a harrowing moment. That wound would never heal, never regrow.

At the time, I accepted it as an inevitability.

A few months later, on an occasion when I hadn't been able to catch a decent meal in days, I foolishly chased a man into a building supplies store. I was frantic and sluggish, as all zombies are, after not eating for long periods of time.

I could smell my catch and it was tantalizing, mouth-watering, I shut my eyes…

And he smacked me across the head with a shovel.

I fell, possibly fractured my jaw—although it's hard to tell—it was already hanging at a funny angle before that. Worst of all, my ear flew off with the swing.

I watched it sail through the air and land smack into a planter as though he'd aimed and I was over taken by rage. The man didn't stand a chance.

His brain was more than satisfying. It rushed me and made me lucid and strong at the same time. It was then, in the throes of TBE that I had my revelation.

It was haste that damaged me every time. Losing my cool, chasing people down, trying to fight when I was frantic for food and not thinking clearly.

The solution then, *must be* to remain regularly fed and to approach getting your next meals with a little *finesse*.

The most important thing to do was stop chasing. If someone ran, I let them go.

You must try with all of your might to *let them go*.

It may seem ridiculous. At the beginning, you may not even be able to, that's okay. Just try again the next time.

The key to success is repetition and…

STEP 3:

Feed regularly.

I know what you're thinking, *how can I feed regularly when I'm letting people go?*

It's a hard fact to accept, but these chases do more than just rough us up—they also tire us out. All the zombies I've ever known have fed and then rested. For days. Until they were starving again.

That's what I use to do. Now though, I've devised something of a routine that keeps me going and keeps me from ever getting to that state of starvation.

The tricks to doing that involve...

Integrating into living society

My first try at reintegration into the "living" world was an attempt at STEP 3, feeding regularly.

I went to the butcher.

He was a nice man named Randy, who I use to visit in life before I became a vegetarian a few years back. I remembered that he had fantastic cuts and after my revelation about feeding, I decided to pay him a visit.

It was my first time trying to communicate with a person since the incident with Sally. I admit that I was nervous.

I entered the shop through the front door. The bell rang, alerting the staff and customers to my arrival.

All eyes turned to me.

Someone screamed.

Everyone ran.

Except for Mr. Randy.

He fell back against the wall behind the counter, shrinking away from me, sucking in his large belly, his small eyes widened in fear.

A small thread of guilt actually swept through me. The first I had felt since transitioning and I could only assume it was because my mind wasn't overtaken by hunger.

I ignored the feeling though, and since he hadn't yet run out the back door, I did my best to communicate with him.

At the time, I'd already figured out that forming words was too hard. Instead, I pointed at the meat and grunted.

Mr. Randy let out a little squeaky noise.

I pointed to my own head, then my mouth.

"Uh, Uh."

He frowned but still didn't move, frozen in fear.

Frustrated, I pointed at the meat and then at my own head. This time, he followed the gestures.

"Do you want to buy something?" he asked in a small, high voice.

Thank goodness!

I nodded.

Randy sank from the wall, his face a mask of confusion.

I pointed at my head again and his eyes widened.

"Brains?" he asked hesitantly.

Yes!

"Yrrrrrrrrrr!"

He stared at me.

"Huh…"

Finally as though startled awake, he began to look up and down the cooler and then shook his head.

TIP

It may take a few tries at a few different butcher shops (especially depending on your level of communication and decay) but once you find one that understands you, you'll be surprised how eager he will be to keep you eating cow brains instead of human brains. It's like a good deed for the person, a total win/win scenario.

"Wait, what am I doing, we don't sell brains."

I let out a frustrated sound and he gave me an indignant look.

"Just wait a minute, I might have some in the back."

I waited as patiently as I could, wondering if it would work and hoping that he had some.

A moment later he emerged, carrying a little bundle in his gloved hands.

He wrapped it all up in a little paper package and weighed it.

"It's veal brain," he said, taping it up. "Is that okay?"

I shrugged and took the offered package.

I knew I didn't have money, but instinctively I reached into my purse, searching. I pulled out an empty pocket and gave him a helpless look.

Randy chuckled.

"It's on me," he said. Then as I was leaving the shop, "Come again!"

I managed to get out the door before examining the package.

It was wrapped securely but I took a big whiff. The tantalizing allure of brain was too much for me to resist.

I ate the entire thing.

I tried to rip the paper out of the way but a lot of it ended up in my mouth. And I got TBE. It hadn't even been a day since my last feeding and the renewed buzz from the second brain took me to a whole new level.

Yes, animal brain is different to human brain. It's not *as* effective, but it is more readily available. It's easier to get your hands on, especially if you establish a relationship with your butcher, like I managed to do.

Since then, I eventually weened completely off of human brain. They're just too much effort and energy wasted in attempting to catch them. There's also something about catching humans I'm not too fond of—the mess—obviously.

I now consider myself a zombie vegetarian.

But that is just the first, in a long line of things you may want to do, in order to integrate into society.

TIP

The main goal of all of this is to become non-threatening to those who surround you. If they don't think you will act out and kill, they may be more inclined to help you and/or *at least* not attack you.

Here are some more things you can do;

1) Keep groaning and grunting to a minimum.

2) If someone greets you with a wave or hello. Just nod.

3) For other forms of communicating, body language goes a long way.

4) For long periods of rest, keep in places that are fairly open. Don't rest behind a door where people may think you are planning to jump out from.

5) Maintain a bit of a routine. The more often people see you about, the more quickly they will get use to your presence.

If you are planning to continue to eat human brains every few days on a normal schedule, make sure that you don't eat people in *any* of the areas where you interact. That will ruin all of your hard work. Humans won't forget that you killed someone they know. Keep your neighborhood and your hunting ground separate!

Remember, when you *do* hunt, don't over exert yourself. You will be amazed at how effective hiding quietly will be. If you can exercise patience (with the help of a little animal brain on the side) then unsuspecting people will simply walk right into your waiting trap.

A few good places to try are;

-Abandoned gas stations

-Corn fields

-Car parks

-Fair grounds

Another point to consider is to refresh your clothing. Sprucing yourself up can go a long way in helping you integrate, as well as helping you with your self-esteem. *But for more details on personal care, check out chapters four and five.*

Some of you may find of all of this too overwhelming. Maybe you *like* hunting people and don't care if they trust your presence.

If that is how you think, just keep in mind that—aside from falling apart more quickly—the zombies who are hunted down, shot or burned, are the ones who make a big scene killing in public.

If you decide to carry on with those acts, make sure that you do so *very* carefully and discreetly. Don't end up as a public display as you are "put out" by hunters.

Believe it or not, I have already addressed...

See how easy getting all of this down can be?

Alternative choices are simply options *other than the obvious ones.*

For example, choosing to hunt, by waiting in a clever location, is an alternative choice to joining zombie mobs and chasing people down in the open. Choosing to eat animal brain to sustain lucidity is an alternative choice to constantly hunting humans.

Being different from the average zombie, is an alternative choice. And if you want to succeed in the afterlife, being different is *the right choice.*

In every moment, before proceeding with an action, practice asking this question; **should I make this choice, or an *alternate choice?***

If your answer is *yes* and you are harmed or maimed permanently, at least you will have no regrets. At least you will be able to take responsibility for your actions and accept the outcome. Otherwise, you may always carry the regret of carrying out a simple, thoughtless action.

With all the praise that I am giving to animal brains you may ask yourself this very valid questions. **Why reintegrate into society at all? Why not remain in the wild and feed on the creatures there?**

Dangers of the Wild

Many zombies do just that. They prowl the wilds. Fields, forests and deserts all around the world are their hunting grounds. They feed on any animals they can catch and on any person unlucky enough to be stranded in their midst.

I won't pretend to be an expert on this matter. I've always been a city girl. But my observations are *not* in favor of this lifestyle. For one, the zombies in these areas often seem to be stranded and lost, themselves. Not to mention that food is *very* hard to come by. If it was easy to come by, why are these zombies the most reckless and hungry, the most eager to attack any person to feed? *Clearly they are starving.*

Yes, there are lots of animals around but with a mind clouded by hunger, it's not very easy to catch anything, let alone a nimble, wild animal. Of course that doesn't apply to everyone, but I believe that the butcher is a much easier way to meet your animal brain needs.

And on this topic, there is another *major* thing to consider; wild animals get hungry too. And we are hard to resist.

In this city alone, I have already lost an entire finger to crows. I have peck marks in the back of my skull that make my hair a constant mess. I have been chased by dogs, stalked by pigeons and a stray kitty cat nearly finished me.

Imagine the animals in the *wild*. Coyotes and hawks and bears and countless other animals that would be all too happy to eat you right up. Imagine what might be left of you, still living...

That is *not* the way to unlive an enjoyable afterlife!

CHAPTER THREE - Walk don't Run

What you will learn in this chapter
✓ How to conserve energy and preserve your body longer
✓ How long can we last?
✓ Dealing with the smell
✓ No Baths!

How to conserve energy and preserve your body longer

So far, we've learned how to use alternate methods to hunting and we have concentrated on keeping the mind lucid and active. We have concentrated on learning how to think *before* acting and how to use humans—not just as a meal—but to help you.

The reason all of this is important is because it all relates directly to the *length and quality of your afterlife.*

Simply put, the more you waste your energy, the more you lose literal pieces of yourself, the shorter and more difficult your afterlife will be.

Aside from what we have already learned, here are some very important ways to keep yourself unliving for a longer time.

1) Keep cool

It's a simple fact that flesh keeps longer if it is kept chilled. Like meat in your refrigerator. If you are staying mostly somewhere cold, like an underground car park, then you are already far ahead of the crowd. If you are from a cold place then you also have an upper hand.

For myself, instead of having to move somewhere cold like—shudder—*Canada,* I started to spend long hours at the mall. The AC there is a lovely cool temperature and I get to stay up to date on current trends. Not to mention, that it also created something of a social environment for me, which I will get to later.

2) Stay in doors

As much as possible. I doesn't need to be a constant thing. Of course you can go outside but the less exposure you have to the elements, the better. Think of how the wind and rain can erode stone and metal. How the sun can melt plastic and start fires. If we are constantly outdoors, the effects will begin to show. We will become ranker and more brittle than other zombies who stay mostly away from the elements.

3) Groom

This may make you raise a brow, but clipping nails and hair for a start, will help you in ways you won't expect. Hair that is too long and wild gets caught and pulled more often. And you never want to pull on loose flesh, like ours. Likewise, nails can scratch and leave permanent marks that can get worse later. They can also split and break if they get long enough, causing great discomfort.

4) Rest regularly

Don't just collapse from exhaustion half way across the street, still trying to get somewhere. We've all been there. It's not pleasant. Instead, try to take proper

TIP

If you must be outside, choose locations with lots of shade and choose days that are lovely and cool, with no rain or snow.

naps at times when you feel safe and full. You'll be surprised to learn that sleep can still recharge you and be a pleasurable experience.

5) Stay clean

Cleanliness can actually help keep your body fresh for longer! I bet you never thought that was possible, but it's true. Staying clean is the absolute best way to stop our open wounds from festering, and nasty infections from growing. All that green puss? Don't just embrace it. Get rid of it.

How long can we last?

Realistically, a zombie is only meant to exist about double the remaining life their living body had in them. So considering that I was twenty seven at my death, I have a possibility of unliving upwards of 120 years.

Sounds ridiculous, I know.

Has any zombie ever lived for that long? I've never heard of one doing it. Of course, there have also been no tests done on the subject, as of yet. It is still a mysterious area of science.

My personal belief is that the science is right. But until now, no zombies ever gave the science a chance, choosing instead to run amok, losing body parts everywhere they go.

We can be the wave of zombies that last well beyond what people expect.

We can be the test subjects for zombies everywhere!

I know it sounds dramatic, but since strictly implementing my rules, my degeneration has all but stopped. I can't say that it has gone backwards. I'll never be alive again, but at the time that I am writing this, it has been two years since I first transitioned and aside from the parts that I already told you, I have not lost or seriously injured *any* body part.

That's right.

It's been nearly two years and I am still, almost perfectly, preserved.

I bet now you are paying close attention.

Dealing with the Smell

If you still *have* a sense of smell, you are most likely use to the stench of rot that follows you around.

But that doesn't make it okay.

A big part of what we are trying to do is to learn to remain closely involved in "living" society and the smell of death makes it surprisingly difficult to do that.

When I first chose the mall as my destination, people actually ran from me. Shops I entered, emptied immediately and wherever I went, there was a radius around me that — aside from the zombie that kept to the mall parking lot — no one would enter. For a while, I thought it was because people were scared of me.

Then I realized that it was the smell.

It gave me away anywhere I went, long before I was seen.

This was a problem that I had never even considered.

How could I keep clean and maybe even smell like I wasn't dead?

There are some simple things that I tried, that really helped the matter.

My experimentation began in the ladies washroom.

The first discovery I made was immediate and exciting.

Many public washrooms have sensors for their taps. There was no difficult maneuvering required to turn the tap. I simply held my hands under the faucet and water poured out.

I managed to splash myself and then pat dry as best I could with some paper towel.

That was okay for a first try. It didn't accomplish much but at the time, I was quite happy with it.

The next day, I managed to take paper towel first, wet it and then rub the wet paper towel over myself.

This was much more effective and that day, when I strolled the mall or sat on one of the benches, people walked much closer to me before realizing that I was there.

It wasn't enough though.

Over the rest of the month, through hard work, I managed to develop a routine

TIP

Don't scrub yourself with anything hard, like a loofa or a rough towel. That could seriously damage or remove your skin.

that makes my undead smell, nearly non-existent.

First, I "acquired" a soft sponge from one of the bath shops, along with a towel and body wash. I didn't really want to steal, but none of the staff seemed to want to stop me. They watched me take the stuff uneasily. I waved on my way out the door as a thank you. I consider it a gift.

After that, I carefully removed my clothing.

My technique was to wet the sponge and apply soap to it. Rub that gently over my body, using extreme care around wounds. Then to wash out the soap from the sponge and do the same thing again to remove the soap.

Afterwards, I patted dry with the towel to make sure that no damp areas remained.

I realized then that my clothes were in serious need of washing, but there was nothing I could do.

I pulled my skirt and tank top back on, followed by my pumps (the heel on one, long gone) and addressed myself in the mirror.

I still looked *very* undead, but at least I looked like a lovely, clean, fresh corpse.

I stepped out into the mall, amidst a crowd of shoppers.

I still expected the people to clear out of my way but no one did.

One or two people who looked straight at me and realized what I was, jumped away from me, startled, but no one else really took any notice.

It was an exciting moment. If our hearts could beat, mine would have been pounding from the accomplishment.

TIP

Be very careful around wounds and make sure you are prepared to spend up to three hours on the process. It can be frustrating, especially dressing and undressing, but keep at it and you will succeed!

How to clean yourself: summary
Find a public washroom that you can easily access with automatic sinks.
Remove your clothing.
Wet a sponge or paper towel with soap and water.
Very gently dab soap and water over your entire body.
Wash soap out of sponge OR get fresh paper towel and wet it.
Again, very gently dab your entire body to remove soap.
Get fresh paper towel OR get dry towel.
Very gently pat yourself dry.
Put clothes back on.

If you do get wet, find something to pat yourself dry with as soon as you can. Paper towels, rags, etc. If possible, change your clothes or remove them and allow them to dry before putting them back on.

No Baths!

I know, I know, bathing just seems so much easier. Why not just find water and jump in, get everything, including your clothes clean?

Well, maybe that's an option for *some* zombies. You know, the ones with blow dryers for their hair, dryers for their clothes and towels to dry off every other part of their bodies too.

Yeah right.

For rotting flesh to be submerged in water... it's just never good. **Think about it.**

If you don't want to be preserved at all, go for it. If you *do* want to last, don't dunk yourself in water. *Ever.* It just makes it worse. Also, stay away from rain.

Sponge baths, soap and clean clothes are definitely the best bet to keeping fresh. (More about clothes in *chapter five, fashion dos and don'ts.*)

TIP

Perfume can be a good thing but sometimes it mingles with our smell in entirely the wrong way! I suggest air fresheners instead. Fabric fresheners are also excellent. And both have a variety of scents to pick from.

CHAPTER FOUR - Goodbye Eye

What you will learn in this chapter;
✓ Identifying *why*
✓ Avoiding making the same mistake twice
✓ Losing body parts; how to cope

Identifying why

It can be a hard pill to swallow. You lost something important. You lost a part of yourself. *Literally*. And it's never coming back.

It can make you lash out. It can make you reckless. It can make you grieve, in the only way that you can.

I understand all too well. I've lost my fair share of body parts and it's never easy. It's the whole reason I began this journey of self-preservation, in search of happiness.

Really, the only consistent thing we've had in our existence is the fact that we have lived or unlived it in these fleshy vessels. We have slept, fed, grown or fallen apart all in the same skin. It is a representation of us. *And what does it say about us, if we are in pieces?*

This isn't an easy subject.

For this chapter, I can't give you a solid solution. It is a journey that we must all make on our own, but I can offer my advice on how to move on with a bright new outlook.

As with any problem, the first thing that one must do is ask themselves *why*. Now I'm not talking some melodramatic *why me*, type of thing, but why *exactly* did this happen?

Be precise.

Were you careless? Did you walk out in front of a car? Did you fall down a staircase, like I did?

Be even more specific than that. *Why did you fall down the staircase?*

When I asked myself that question, there were two answers. One—which we have already addressed—I was so hungry, I wasn't being careful. I already found a solution to that with the butcher shop.

But there was something else that I had over looked. I was in heels. I had been in—what use to be—gorgeous pumps, with a platform base. Almost as soon as I'd transitioned, one of my heels had broken off.

Like most undead, I did not remove the shoes. Some might argue that it's best to keep shoes on if we want to keep our feet, no matter how rough the shoes are. That is absolutely right, of course. But I was hobbling around for months, chasing people down with one heel intact and one broken off. It is a wonder I didn't fall more often.

If you have the specific answer as to why it happened, that is the only way to prevent making the same mistake twice.

Avoid making the same mistake twice

This can be tricky. It depends on the individual and on the mistake itself.

If the mistake is serious enough (laying across an active train track, for example) then you may never have the chance to learn from your mistakes.

There are some easy fixes though.

My immediate solution for my shoes was to snap the other heel off.

With the shape of my shoes, I had to walk at a funny angle with my feet kind of pointing up at the toes. But at least it was the same on both feet and much easier to manage that way.

For me, it worked.

If you have similar problems, untied laces for example, consider just tucking them in to the sides of your shoes, to avoid tripping.

Whatever the mistake was that cost you your flesh, spend time trying to fix the problem and you will feel your confidence return to you.

Losing body parts; how to cope

I suppose it's hard to say *'the damage is done, learn from your mistakes and move on.'*

I would hate to hear that myself and although, in a lot of ways it may be true, that is not what I am trying to say.

The truth is that these things do happen, especially to us. And though it may be hard, though you may feel like no one understands you just because you cannot speak, that does not mean that you are alone.

It's hard to experience any sort of loss or disability. At least the living can often be healed, while we cannot. It doesn't seem fair.

In reality though, right now, we are meant to be dead. Completely dead, not just half dead. We could have remained unmoving and cold, but that didn't happen—well, we are still cold actually, but this unlife that we have here, right now, it's special. It's a gift.

It's a little extra time that others aren't given.

Don't you think that we should embrace it? If we are meant to be undead, then we aren't *meant* to be all in one piece. The two go hand in hand.

Maybe this is the universe's way of trying to teach us that we are more than just our physical bodies. Maybe right now, missing an arm or both legs or more, we are still more whole then we ever were in "life".

It's something to think about.

Yes, it hurts to lose something that you are used to having. But does it make you any less of a zombie?

I think it makes you a better one.

"Wanting to be someone else is a waste of the person you are."

Marilyn Monroe

CHAPTER FIVE—Fashion Do's and Don'ts

What you will learn in this chapter;
✓ Does it still matter?
✓ Finding the new you.

Does it still matter?

As a child, I learned that my physical appearance tied in directly to how I was feeling. Have you ever heard the saying *to be beautiful, surround yourself with beautiful things*? To me that always included clothes and accessories. See, it's like this; if you are surrounded by beauty, you feel beautiful and beyond that, if you believe that you *look* good, you *feel* good too.

There's no denying the effect.

Even by sprucing up in the mall's public washroom, I suddenly felt a little bit like my old self again. Not that I *want* to be Cassidy Heart ever again, but I was reminded of the fundamental things that really *meant* something to me.

I felt that I looked good—pretty *damn* good—for a zombie and so I *felt* damn good, too.

I'm sure that you will feel the effects the first time you clean yourself up with my techniques. So why not take it to the next level? **Why not make yourself the very best version of you, right now?**

I'm not at all saying that you should try to look like your old self, that'll never happen. But why not look like the very best zombie on the block?

The worst that can happen is nothing, the best that can happen is you can feel good about yourself and gain some confidence.

TIP: You'll never look like you did before and no one might appreciate the changes you make now, but this is for *you*. So that you can think about yourself and have some *fun* being undead. Let's get your mind off surviving and have fun!

Finding the new you

This is the fun part. This is the part that really matters in starting a new life.

It's time to shed the old you.

Are you still stuck on the little habits that you carried around with you in life? Do you still carry around a briefcase? Do you frequently return to your old bar?

Why?

There it is again, that infamous question. You must hate it by now because it causes the most confusion and anguish.

But there is an important reason for this question. If you ask yourself *why*, and the answer is because you truly love that bar's atmosphere and that briefcase is a perfect tool for head bashing, then you are still being true to yourself and you should keep up those habits!

But if you ask yourself *why* and the answer is *just* that it is a habit, then it is time to *let go*. If you don't truly enjoy what you are doing, but you do it anyway, without any thought as to your reasoning, then it's not good.

You carry that briefcase because you *can't* let it go? You visit that bar because you *can't* stay away?

Similar to being addicted, don't you think?

I get it. I carried my purse around for ages, not to mention that I kept those damn heels on.

I didn't want to entertain the idea of being someone else. I liked being Cassidy Heart, I didn't want her life to truly be over. Maybe I thought that changing my persona would really bring an end to her and I just wasn't ready.

But you are *not* your outfit. You are *not* your habits or your routine.

If thinking these things through causes headaches or intense rampaging, take a break. Don't think about it for a little while. Forget about the task until you feel comfortable and confident and then return to the question only when you are ready. But remember, running from the problem won't help to fix it or change your life. Be sure to come back to the hard questions when you can.

It is okay to change how you look or behave, because no matter what, you will always be you.

Why not have some fun with it?

Consider two things, what do you like? What do you need?

If you like platforms and heels, like me, sadly, it just won't work. They're too hard to stay steady in.

Other things that won't work are;

- Overalls
- Body suits
- Snow pants
- Suspenders
- Shoes with laces
- Lots of buttons
- Anything too tight

> TIP
>
> An alternative to heels are fancy flats. Find some glittery or shiny shoes and you won't feel like you are missing out.

You can see where I am going with this. You have to find something that you like, that **A)** won't be too hard to put on and **B)** won't cause any accidents while putting them on, taking them off, or wearing them.

Need some new clothes? Try one of the donations boxes sure to be around any city. You will be surprised with the quality and variety of things available. Ransack as many as you need in order to find the perfect outfit for *you*.

You'd be surprised though, given the limitations I listed, just how many nice things we can still wear.

Myself, I found a loose white dress and sparkly flats that were easy to slip into. And yes, before you ask, I finally ditched the purse.

I tend to wear each of my outfits for as long as three to four weeks before discarding the soiled clothing in exchange for another outfit.

Some other things I tried were loose pants and a long sleeved shirt. It hid my ruined arm nicely and I felt helped me to blend in more by hiding more of my skin, but the outfit just wasn't me.

Now, I tend to look for loose, long sleeve dresses that still show a little bit of leg.

On a side note, some of the mall employees who have gotten to know me over time, now give me the odd little gifts to add to my look. Things like scarves or jackets. They donate to *me* now instead of to other charities. This is just a small example of how it can help to integrate.

TIP

Don't be afraid to try something new! You might be surprised at just how much you like it.

CHAPTER SIX - 'Till Decomposition Do Us Part

What you will learn in this chapter;
✓ How to make friends
✓ Dating. Do or Don't?
✓ How to maintain a meaningful relationship

How to make friends

First of all, don't bother trying to rekindle old relationships. Those who couldn't accept you deceased, are clearly not the best people to have as friends anyway.

What I am talking about here, is how to make *brand new friends*.

It may seem impossible now but it is easier than you may think.

Just like anything else, you must take it in simple steps.

1) **Make eye contact** – this is essential in finding someone who will respond to you. Don't be discouraged if you are ignored. Your friendliness might be shocking to some.

2) **Use some form of acknowledgment** – my technique is always to nod. It works for me. Some other ways are; to wave, to smile, or to bow.

3) **Communicate about something you have in common** – it can be tricky until you get the hang of it but soon you will find that it is easier than you thought. A simple way to start, would be to point at something and shake or nod your head in disgust or appreciation. Your chosen zombie, or human, will likely respond.

4) **Practice!** – keep these tips going and the more often you communicate with the same individuals the sooner you will be on your way to having new friends!

As with everything, I speak from experience. It took me several months before I actually saw any results of my actions.

The first to properly respond to me was the zombie who stays mostly in the car park below the mall.

Desperate for someone to "talk" to, I decided to pay him a visit.

He was slim, dressed in a faded, moldy suit with a ridiculous pair of broken glasses *still* on his face—see what I mean about silly habits? My guess was that he was a banker or tax man in life.

If we were both still living, I probably wouldn't have given him a second glance. But now, we were both in a similar position and both living in more or less the same location.

He was laying across one of the parking spots when I found him. Fast asleep, like a corpse.

He looked up only as I reached him, fixing his bespectacled gaze on me.

I'd heard he ate the occasional mall goer, but he seemed harmless enough to me.

For a while we stared at each other.

Although I had already been practicing at that point, I still found the whole communicating thing awkward and nerve-wracking when there was nothing to say.

Convinced I was just there to stare at him, he rested his head back down on the cool cement and I panicked.

"Uhhhhhhhhhhhhh."

He looked at me again, expectantly.

Unsure what else to do, I waved at him. He gave me an odd look and then, waved back.

I was elated.

This time, when he laid back down, I let him return to his nap. But I came back the next day.

We gave our little waves and he continued the conversation by pointing at a kid who skate boarded by and shaking his head in disgust.

I nodded agreement.

The day after that, I didn't go down to the lot. I was planning to, but I was a bit tired and I needed to make another trip to the butcher shop.

I returned to the mall and sat on a bench overlooking the fountain while I ate.

A scream drew my attention to *him*, the parking-lot-tax-zombie, casually stumbling through the mall and knocking into people that he didn't seem too interested in.

He was fixated on me. He didn't slow or take his eyes off of me, until he was standing right at my bench. Then he looked away and shifted awkwardly.

I was very touched by the effort that he put in.

I patted the seat next to me and he took the invitation, sitting quietly at my side.

After a moment I even offered him some brain from my packet.

He shoved his face into it ravenously and ate a bit more than I wanted him to, but I thought it was worth it in exchange for friendship.

We spent the rest of the day taking in the view and making small little "comments" at people passing by.

After that, it became our routine.

Through the 5 steps listed above, I have now managed to collect a group of like-minded zombies and countless humans who treat me favourably.

Be warned that the living are much less receptive than the undead and it can take much longer to win one of them over. That said, it was through this method that I managed to create a community that I am very much a part of. I highly recommend doing the same.

Dating. Do or don't?

To this question I say, *why not?*

Really. You know how people say "you only live once"? *Wrong!* For us anyway, we are already on our second "life". One thing is for certain though. You're only *undead* once. Can you imagine the mess of coming back *again?*

I don't even want to think about it.

All I know is that, when parking lot-tax zombie approached me with a flower one day, I took it. Okay, it was a dandelion, and maybe I would never have looked at him twice before, but one of the beautiful things about being undead is that really quickly, you learn how little looks are important. You stop judging, because no one unliving is perfect, yourself included.

He came to me again, the next day with a cute charm bracelet. I don't know where he got it, nor do I care. It's the thought that counts.

Then, as though I needed more convincing, he brought me a ring the next day.

It was plastic, from one of the quarter machines, but the fact that he had somehow managed to put a quarter in and turn the handle... it nearly brought a tear to my eye.

Before agreeing, the only thing that I really needed was simple.

I pointed to myself.

"BRUUUGGGHHHHH," I said.

He didn't get my meaning and stared at me blankly so I repeated the action.

Understanding crossed his face and he pointed at himself.

"ERRRRRRRHHHHHH," he moaned.

Names out of the way, I took the ring and his hand and we have been going steady ever since.

How to maintain a meaningful relationship

Our relationship, has given me more happiness, support and comfort, than anything that I left behind in my old life.

A big part of the reason for that, is because we don't judge each other.

A lot of living and undead alike, seem to think that the ideas in this book are farfetched. A zombie that doesn't eat people's brains? A zombie that bathes?

Truthfully, if you are not willing to try *everything* you can, in order to make a change, then this all may seem ridiculous to you.

But ERRRRRRRHHHHHH never judged me.

He supported me. He hung out in the mall with me. He went with me to the donations boxes, even though he didn't need to.

Eventually, he started to get his own packets of animal brains on our trips to the butchers.

He compromised for me and supported me and in return, I did the same.

I spent nights in the car park with him, even though it was damp down there. I didn't say anything about his glasses.

Eventually, he started to see the appeal of changing his lifestyle to what I was trying to build, all on his own.

He lost the glasses without me ever pointing them out and now, he spruces up his look every now and then with new-more casual-outfits that suit his new lifestyle.

And as his excitement grew, he came up with new, innovative ideas that I never would have come up with on my own, like the support group and zombie dinners.

If you are in a position where it is possible to have a friendship or partner of any kind, I highly recommend doing it! At least then you can have someone to try all of these techniques with!

What you will learn in this chapter;
✓ Do we have any rights?
✓ Starting over

Do we have any rights?

What a bizarre position we find ourselves in. Legally, we are dead. But we are still here.

We cannot *physically* do a lot of things that the average, "living" person can do and perhaps worst of all, we cannot *legally* do a lot of things that the average living person can do.

Our houses are still here and our cars and computers, etc. And our families are still here. That can be a good or bad thing. I guess the first thing to address is whether you wrote a will. If so, you know who now owns what use to be yours.

Legally, the truth is that nothing belongs to you anymore, no matter how hard you once worked on getting it.

But, there is no law that states that an undead person *cannot* own anything.

What that means is that, if you are somehow on good terms with your family, consider trying to convince them to put your belongings back into your hands.

This can be difficult. For some, it can be impossible.

I know that most zombies are estranged from their families. If you do want to rekindle the relationship, imagine just how effective this book can be for you.

TIP

If you want to become a part of your family again and they see that you are not eating people, you are clean and you attempt to communicate in a simple way, it can be easier than you think. They do still love you deep down, they just think that now you are different. Show them that you are still you somewhere inside and they will be happy to have you back! Just be sure to practice everything first! An outbreak will ruin your chances of getting close to them!

Sadly, if you did not leave your belongings to anyone and they were claimed by the state, then there is nothing that you can do to get it back.

How do I know this side of it?

I figured that out when ERRRRRRRHHHHHH took me to his condo.

The building was classy even from the outside, and even though neither of us really fit the scene anymore, ERRRRRRRHHHHHH walked in like he owned the place. I followed, trying to match his stride.

"Good day, Mr. Walsh," the doorman greeted, barely looking up.

ERRRRRRRHHHHHH grunted.

We took the elevator up all the way to the thirty-fourth floor. A girl took the ride with us, but her face was glued to her screen and she didn't seem to notice that she was standing casually with two zombies.

I watched her walk away, impressed with the level our bathing, changing and "febreezing" had gotten to.

I was led to a door and ERRRRRRRHHHHHH managed to hit the buzzer.

A moment later, the door swung open.

The woman—who I can only assume was once his wife—screamed, but ERRRRRRRHHHHHH walked right passed her and straight up to a book case. It was shelved with heavy books, all relating to law and it was then that I figured out that ERRRRRRRHHHHHH had once been a lawyer.

He went straight for the book he wanted and pulled it off the shelf, holding it out to the woman.

Together, she and I leaned closer to read the title.

GUIDE TO WILLS AND BENEFICIARIES

Huh.

The woman frowned.

"I don't understand," she said.

He pushed the book into her hands and gestured for her to flip through it. The book was thick and it took a while.

Eventually, the three of us were sitting at the table together, while she flipped carefully through the tomb.

Finally, she flipped a page about half way through and ERRRRRRRHHHHHH pointed, grunting in excitement.

We leaned in close to read.

The subheading read, *Transference of Property to an Undead Individual.*

The woman gave him an incredulous look.

"You want me to give you back your money?" she asked.

ERRRRRRRHHHHHH nodded happily, gesturing around to the condo and then to me and himself.

She scoffed loudly.

"Honey, the only reason I even married you was for the money, why the hell would I hand it back over now?"

ERRRRRRRHHHHHH got angry. It was clear to me, even before his former wife caught on.

A slow rumble started in his chest and then he let out a bellow of rage.

She screamed again, falling from her seat in her haste to get away.

ERRRRRRRHHHHHH went after her.

I did try to stop him, but well, we are zombies after all. Our only chance of getting his belongings back was of course if she signed it all over but that didn't seem all that likely anyway.

Personally, I was touched that he went to such an effort in an attempt at starting our afterlives together.

All it meant was that we would have to carry on, starting from scratch.

Starting over

What a daunting phrase.

But there is good news; you have already started over *and* you have already been through the hard parts.

Dealing with the transition is difficult work. Losing your life *is* something to grieve and it comes with losing friends, family, your home and everything that you are familiar with, aside from your body. And even that doesn't stay.

But as with every big change in life or after, you must be ready for anything and learn to appreciate what you have.

The little things make a bigger difference. Friends, food, home, they all mean more now than ever before.

Keep up the good attitude and fight to continue day to day, and there are always going to be good days sprinkled in with the bad ones.

TIP

Don't dwell on the past. Find a new neighborhood to stalk and new people to befriend. *A fresh start* sounds a lot better than *starting over*. And that's what this is, a fresh start.

CHAPTER EIGHT - Unliving in the Moment

What you will learn in this chapter;
✓ Pros and Cons of this new life
✓ How to unlive happily ever after

Pros and Cons

Is it important to weigh the good and the bad in order to measure your own happiness?

For me, it is. Until I had it all written down in front of me, I never really realized how good I now have it.

PROS	CONS
Not tied down to anything. Job, mortgage, people, etc.	Losing everything you fought hard to build in life
Opportunity for new growth	Forced to change without consent
A new ability to see beyond the physical	Difficulty with motor skills
A chance to revamp your look	Thinking is very slow
Don't need to pay for anything	Loss of old life
Can live however you want, without being judged for it	

In my opinion, the good outweighs the bad here. All of the cons that I listed above, have to do with the one thing that I have repeatedly found to be necessary. It can all be summed up with one little phrase; *let it go.*

Your old life can be something that you think of fondly while truly enjoying your new life.

If you continue to practice, it will truly happen one day and sooner than you think.

TIP

Of course it won't happen overnight. Don't be too hard on yourself. It can be difficult at first, but if you just keep reminding yourself not to dwell on the past and of the good that you now have, it *will* happen for you.

How to unlive happily ever after

A big part of that is to accept what is. As a zombie, there will always be struggles. There will always be something making your afterlife more difficult.

The key is to *accept it, adjust and carry on.*

If you break a leg, for example, see if you can splint it and then carry on with your afterlife.

TIP

To splint a broken bone, first you must set it. That means pulling the limb until the bones snap back together. *Then*, get two hard, straight things. Wooden planks work, as do strong sticks or metal rods. Put one on each side of the broken limb and tie them tightly by wrapping a rope, fabric, or bandage around them.

The same can be said for anything that you do, or try to do.

If your first attempt at making a friend doesn't work, don't get mad and kill the person, just move on to someone else.

Eventually, someone will take your advance.

Carrying out the method that I outlined in chapter six, ERRRRRRRHHHHHH and I scoured the streets, trying our friend making techniques on every zombie that we could find.

The few that responded to us were willing to follow us to the parking garage where we had a feast of brains ready in an attempt to start a little community group.

The first meeting was pure havoc. We had the brains on top of a car, since we had no tables. Needless to say, the car was destroyed, a few of the zombies got in a fight (one lost an eye) and ERRRRRRRHHHHHH really lost his temper at the lack of gratitude, which sent *him* rampaging.

I wasn't deterred though. The next week, at the same time, I collected the same zombies.

They followed eagerly, knowing that food awaited.

And it was just as much of a disaster as the first week.

The third week though, there was a break through. Everyone ate eagerly, but there were no fights, the car remained intact and we all began to communicate in our way.

Every week, we carried on with the group and the level of communication grew as the new zombies got the hang of it.

Eventually, one of the local churches opened up their event rooms for us. We are now on the monthly schedule, listed every week as the **Zombie Support Group**. Now, the others have started to bring friends and it continues to grow from there. We hold the occasional parties and two of the original members have branched out to start their own groups in different locations.

Now I have a purpose. I have a new group of girl friends who are much cooler than my last ones. PRIIIIIIIE, UNGGGG and FFFTH are always happy to see me, bringing me snacks and going out of their way to take me to their favourite spots for picnics. Even if they could speak, I don't think they'd ever say anything bad about anyone.

And I have ERRRRRRRHHHHHH, the undead man that I am happy to curl up next to in the stairwell every night. The undead man that I was given a second chance at "living" to find.

This community that we built, all of it, came from a willingness to work hard and change our afterlives.

For me, more specifically, it came from sitting in that stairwell, all that time ago, when I was faced with the choice to embrace this second life or allow myself to waste away, defeated.

I am happy to say that I chose to embrace it. I thoroughly hope that you choose to do the same.

Wow, I gave you a lot to think about, I know. And with our brains…

Let's just say that I'm guessing it took you just as long to read this book as it did for me to write it. And I have an editor who greatly helps by cleaning up the phrasing and typos.

It's no secret that we can't do everything we use to be able to do. Maybe I would have been able to type on my own once, but I never had such an important message to share back then.

Going through these struggles has made me the zombie that I am today. I can say that I have more drive, more confidence in myself as a being and I am more proud of myself than ever before.

Now I can say, my name is BRUUUGGGHHHHH and I am proud to be a zombie.

Practicing the techniques in this book, can you do the same?

Summary of what we learned

1. Zombies are created with voodoo, demonic plagues and/or infections
2. A zombie is an undead individual, whose body continues to parish at a much slower rate than a fully dead individual, due to our regeneration process
3. We crave brain as a meal *and* as a means to gain lucidity
4. To make valid choices, we must always be well fed
5. You must choose the type of afterlife you want to live
6. Chasing meals, leads to injuries
7. A way to be well fed, is to establish a relationship with a local butcher
8. Do what you can to seem unthreatening
9. Wild animals are not our friends
10. Use more subtle ways of hunting in order to sneak up on your prey and avoid injuries
11. It is important to keep your body cool, rested and clean
12. Sponge baths are the best way to stay fresh and remove odor

13. Changing clothes often helps keep you smelling clean
14. Avoid bodies of water
15. Identify the problem that caused an injury in order to avoid making the same mistake twice
16. Sometimes, losing body parts is unavoidable
17. Fashion is important in keeping us feeling good
18. Specific types of clothes suit zombies
19. Steps to getting friends are as simple as making eye contact and starting a "conversation"
20. Dating is still in the picture!
21. Responding to your partner and leaving all judgments behind, lead to a meaningful relationship
22. We are able to reclaim our properties *but* it is very unlikely
23. Starting fresh can lead to bigger, better things
24. There are both pros and cons but I prefer the pros!
25. Unliving happily ever after is still possible!

TIP

Why not spread the word? If you have all of these techniques down, why not start your own Zombie Support Group? I am sure there is a need for one in your community.

If that's not for you, check out the local church/mosque/synagogue/etc. schedules. There is a possibility that there is already a group in your area, looking to help zombies just like you!

ACKNOWLEDGEMENTS

First and foremost, to ERRRRRRRHHHHHH for being so supportive during long hours at the library, banging on the keyboard. For bringing me food and reading my first draft with enthusiasm. I never would have had the guts to submit to publishers if it wasn't for him.

To the community for being able to overlook our looks and let us into their lives. For allowing us to gather and have our groups and grow our own community.

To Djinn Publishing, for overlooking the state of the draft that I sent them. I was unable to edit on my own and they saw the importance of my message and stuck with me, editing my words and my story until it was *exactly* what I was trying to say. I will forever be grateful.

ABOUT THE AUTHOR

BRUUUGGGHHHHH is a lovely, undead woman from LA who has redirected her afterlife to helping other zombies. She is a role model in her community and has been changing the afterlife scene into something fun and social and manageable.

Her dream is for Zombies to be considered a part of society that belongs there, just like any other people out there.

To keep up to date, follow her on twitter @BRUUUGGGHHHHH

Fashion do/don't

I learned youngthat looopk goodmeans feelsgod. Cloths andaccessoriessTo me always.important.

Even in bathroom cleaning males me feels so beter like me ebfore. Now I remember whatisimportantcassidy HeartNot that I *want* to be Cassidy Heart.

Ilooked so good for a zombie andI feeldamn good.

You;;ll feelgood too to use my techniques. Why not take it to thee next level>? Why not make you the besst ofyou?

Not to say to look like youe oldyou. That cantbe.but still look like thebestyiy. The worst that happens is nothing, the best hapiness andconfidenc.

But youwontever beeeeeeeeeeeeeeeeeeeeeeeee like old uou but at least ahev funnow.

ItTime to shedold you.Are youstuck onhabits that you carried with you in life? Do you still holdyour briefcase? Do you still gooto same old bar?

Whty?

This questionyou   must hate it now because it ismost confuzion and anguizzh.

But there iz reason for uestion. Iou ask yourself *why*, BUTthe answer is because you lovlove that bar's

atmosphere and that briefcase is a peeeeeeeeeeeeeerrrrrrrrrrrrrrrrrrfect tool for head BASH!!!!!!!!!!!!!!!!!!!!!!1, then you are still being true KEEPgoing

But if you *why* andtheanswer is *just* habit, then it is time to let go. If you don'tlikewhatyoudo,but you do itwithout brain. That bad.

 You carrybriefcase because you can't let go? You visit the bar because you can't be away?

You addICted?

Yesme toooootooo purse.

Didn't;liketheideai of not beingcassidy. Ididn t want to say foogbye

But youarE NOT clothes.

Changing good.

We shouldhave some fuun

do you like? What you need

If you like highand heels, me too, sad, its not work.

things that won't work, even if ylike them overallsBody suits, dnow pants suspender   shoes with lace. Buttons. Things too tight

Now I wear sh in y shoes no heel.

You know now.. **1** find easy clothes and **2** wont pull skin off. Esy to put on.

THANKS FOR READING, be sure to join our mailing list on www.djinnpublishing.com for upcoming news on the rest of the **Guide to Being Dead** series!